W9-BIA-760

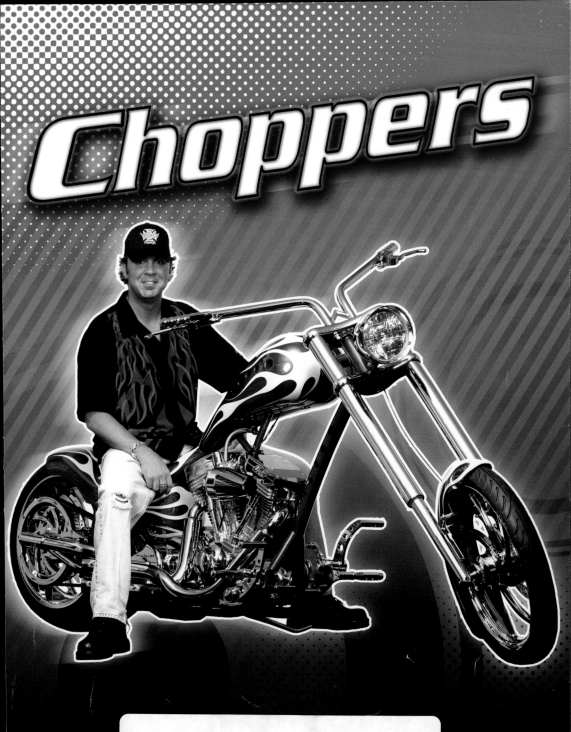

Choppers

BY **JACK DAVID**

TM

Are you ready to take it to the extreme?
Torque books thrust you into the action-packed
world of sports, vehicles, and adventure. These books
may include dirt, smoke, fire, and dangerous stunts.
WARNING: read at your own risk.

Library of Congress Cataloging-in-Publication Data

David, Jack, 1968-
  Choppers / by Jack David.
      p. cm. -- (Torque. Motorcycles)
  Includes bibliographical references and index.
  ISBN-13: 978-1-60014-131-7 (hardcover : alk. paper)
  ISBN-10: 1-60014-131-5 (hardcover : alk. paper)
  1. Motorcycles--Customizing--Juvenile literature. 2. Home-built motorcycles--Juvenile
literature. I. Title.

  TL440.15.D359 2008
  629.227'5--dc22
                                                                              2007014089

This edition first published in 2008 by Bellwether Media.

CONTENTS

WHAT IS A CHOPPER?

A chopper is a type of motorcycle **customized** to have a long and tough look. Owners add, remove, and replace parts to customize their chopper.

Owners move the front tire forward. They add shiny paint jobs. They try to give their bikes a one-of-a-kind look. Choppers are more than vehicles to most owners. A chopper is an expression of its owner's personality.

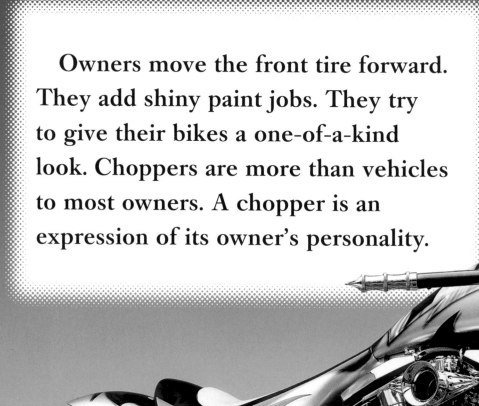

7

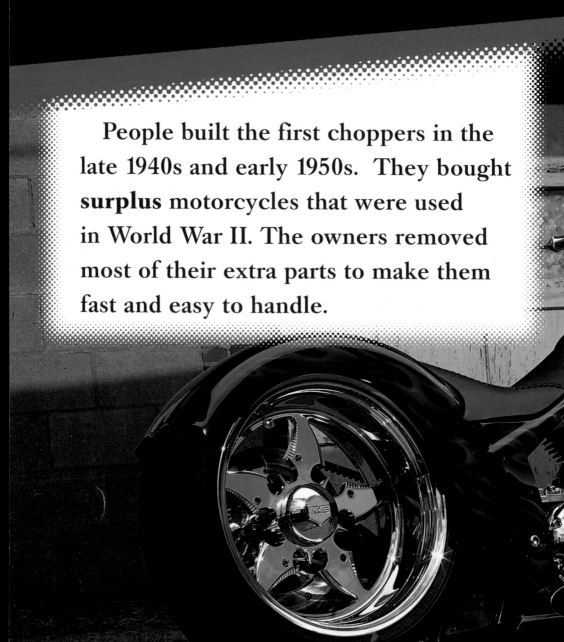

People built the first choppers in the late 1940s and early 1950s. They bought **surplus** motorcycles that were used in World War II. The owners removed most of their extra parts to make them fast and easy to handle.

FAST FACT

CHOPPERS GREW OUT OF A CUSTOMIZING STYLE CALLED "BOBBING."

Classic choppers have a unique look. The front wheel sticks far out in front of the bike. Riders sit low in their seats. They reach up to hold high handlebars.

Almost any type of motorcycle can be turned into a chopper. Harley-Davidson motorcycles are the most popular chopper brand. These American-built bikes are perfect for most chopper fans. They are big, durable, and have powerful engines.

13

FEATURES

A chopper's most unique feature is its long front **fork**. This part holds the bike's front wheel. Owners add extra-long forks to give their choppers a streched-out look.

Owners add many other features to their choppers. Low seats and high handlebars called **ape-hangers** are common. Many owners add a shiny metallic covering called **chrome** to the motorcycle's metal parts. Custom paint jobs, shortened **fenders**, large engines, and other changes complete the look.

FAST FACT

THE FIRST "MODERN CHOPPER" IN THE UNITED STATES WAS BUILT BY WILD CHILD'S CUSTOM SHOP IN KANSAS CITY, MISSOURI.

BUILDING CHOPPERS

Building a chopper is as important as riding it for many owners. Some owners spend years customizing their bikes. They want every detail to be just right. Others buy their choppers from a chopper builder.

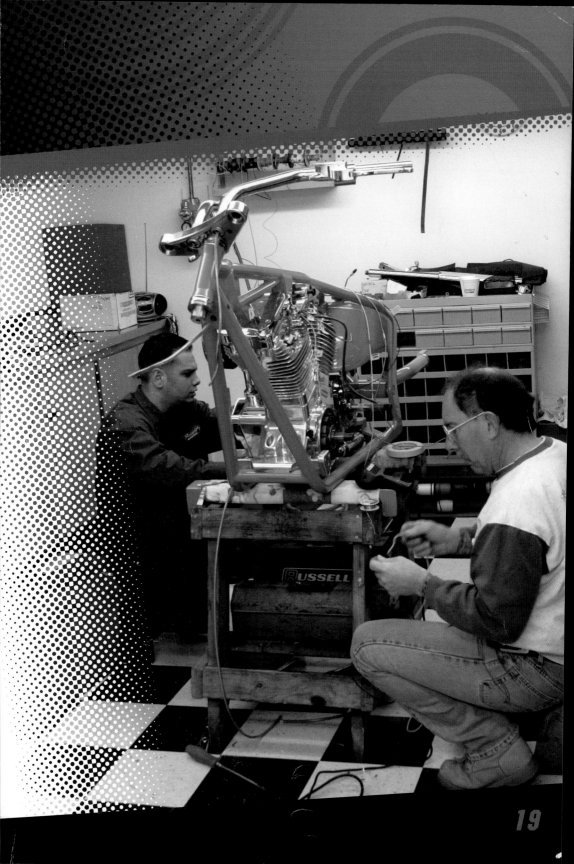

19

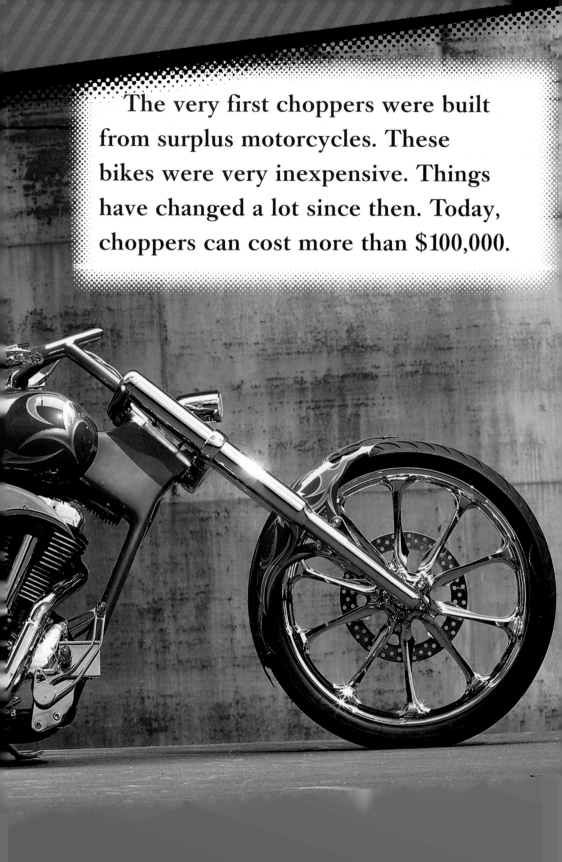

The very first choppers were built from surplus motorcycles. These bikes were very inexpensive. Things have changed a lot since then. Today, choppers can cost more than $100,000.

GLOSSARY

ape-hangers—handlebars with very high grips; riders holding onto ape hangers have their hands close to head level.

chrome—a metallic substance called chromium; chrome gives metal objects a shiny look.

customize—to modify a vehicle to suit one's individual needs

fender—a metal covering over the wheel of a motorcycle

fork—the part of a motorcycle that connects the front wheel to the frame

surplus—more than is needed

TO LEARN MORE

AT THE LIBRARY

Dayton, Connor. *Choppers*. New York: PowerKids Press, 2007.

David, Jack. *Harley-Davidson Motorcycles*. Minneapolis, Minn.: Bellwether, 2007.

Hill, Lee Sullivan. *Motorcycles*. Minneapolis, Minn.: Lerner Publications Co., 2004.

ON THE WEB

Learning more about motorcycles is as easy as 1, 2, 3.

1. Go to www.factsurfer.com

2. Enter "motorcycles" into search box.

3. Click the "Surf" button and you will see a list of related web sites.

With factsurfer.com, finding more information is just a click away.

INDEX